M
P

MW00654522

Edited by
Bart Tesoriero

Nihil Obstat: Right Reverend Archimandrite Francis Vivona,
                  S.T.M., J.C.L.
Imprimatur: Most Reverend Joseph A. Pepe, D.D., J.C.D.
Date: August 4, 2011
                  The Feast of Saint John Marie Vianney

Published with the approval of the
Committee on Divine Worship, United States Conference of Catholic Bishops.

Library of Congress Control Number: 2011909035
ISBN 1-61796-054-3

Copyright 2006, 2011 by Aquinas Press
First Edition, 2006; Second Edition, 2011
Tenth Printing, November, 2015

Table of Contents

Traditional Prayers

The Sign of the Cross

In the name of the Father ✠ and of the Son, and of the Holy Spirit, Amen.

The Lord's Prayer

Our Father, Who art in heaven, hallowed be Thy Name;
Thy Kingdom come;
Thy Will be done on earth as it is in heaven.

Give us this day our daily bread;
and forgive us our trespasses,
as we forgive those who trespass against us;
and lead us not into temptation,
but deliver us from evil.

For the kingdom, the power,
and the glory are Yours now and forever. Amen.

The Hail Mary

Hail Mary, full of grace, the Lord is with thee;
Blessed art thou among women,
and blessed is the fruit of thy womb, Jesus.

Holy Mary, Mother of God, pray for us sinners,
now and at the hour of our death. Amen.

Glory Be to the Father

Glory be to the Father, and to the Son, and to the Holy Spirit; as it was in the beginning, is now, and ever shall be, world without end. Amen.

Act of Faith

O my God, I firmly believe that You are one God in three Divine Persons, the Father, the Son, and the Holy Spirit. I believe in Jesus Christ Your Son, who became man and died for our sins, and who will come to judge the living and the dead. I believe these and all the truths which the Holy Catholic Church teaches, because You have revealed them, who can neither deceive nor be deceived. Amen.

Act of Hope

O my God, trusting in Your infinite goodness and promises, I hope to obtain pardon of my sins, the help of Your grace, and life everlasting, through the merits of Jesus Christ, my Lord and Redeemer. Amen.

Act of Love

O my God, I love You above all things, and with my whole heart and soul, because You are all-good and worthy of all my love. I love my neighbor as myself for love of You. I forgive all who have injured me, and I ask pardon of all whom I have injured. Amen.

Morning Offering to the Sacred Heart

O Jesus, through the Immaculate Heart of
Mary, I offer You my prayers, works, joys and
sufferings of this day: for all the intentions of
Your Sacred Heart, in union with the Holy
Sacrifice of the Mass throughout the world, in
reparation for my sins, for the intentions of all
our associates, and in particular for the intentions
of our Holy Father. Amen.

Daily Consecration to Mary

O Mary, My Queen and my Mother, I give myself entirely to you, and
to show my devotion to you I consecrate to you this day my eyes, my
ears, my mouth, my heart, my whole body without reserve.
Wherefore, good Mother, as I am your own, keep me and guard me
as your property and possession. Amen.

Prayer to Your Guardian Angel

O Angel of God, my Guardian dear,

to whom God's love commits me here,

ever this day (or night) be at my side,

to light and guard, to rule and guide. Amen.

Morning Prayers

It is always good to pray the Acts of Faith, Hope, Charity, and Contrition every morning or evening. It is also a good practice to pray the Litany of the Sacred Heart or of the Holy Name in the morning and that of the Blessed Virgin in the evening.

Upon Rising

O almighty God, thank You for giving me another day in which to serve You. Grant that I may use it to Your honor and glory and to my own salvation. Amen.

While Dressing

O heavenly Father, clothe me with the garment of holiness that I may do Your will today, and preserve me from mortal sin.

Before Beginning the Day's Work

O God, I love You for all Your goodness to me. Help me to show my love for You this day by keeping Your holy law, even when it is most difficult. Keep me from pride and boastfulness. I know well my own weakness and unworthiness, and I beg Your help in all my actions.

Take care of me today, dear Jesus. Send my holy guardian angel to watch over me. Keep me from danger and temptation, but if I must suffer them, help me to do so patiently and with courage. Bless my family and my friends today and give them health and happiness.

O Jesus, through the Immaculate Heart of Mary, I offer You my prayers, works, joys, and sufferings for all the intentions of Your Sacred Heart, in union with the Holy Sacrifice of the Mass throughout the world, for the intentions of all our associates, in particular for the intentions recommended by our Holy Father, the Pope, and for the Holy Souls in Purgatory.

Now that the sun has risen, I humbly pray to You, dear God, to save me from all harm, to help me restrain my tongue and my unruly appetites, and to behave in such a manner that I may not be ashamed to kneel before You tonight and ask Your blessing. O Holy Spirit, take possession of my voice and my intelligence, that they may serve You well. Let peace reign today throughout the world and let hatred be unknown.

> I offer You, dear Jesus,
>   Each action of today;
> My prayers, my works, my sufferings,
>   Accept them now I pray.
>
> I offer You, dear Jesus,
>   O who could offer more,
> Yourself in sweet communion,
>   The Heart that I adore.
>
> And while my heart, dear Jesus,
>   For sinners ever pleads,
> I offer You through Mary
>   A decade of her beads.
>
> Then take my heart, dear Jesus,
>   Take all I have to give.
> O would that I could give my life
>   Within Your Heart to live.
>
> Jesus, Mary, and Joseph,
>   Be with me all the day.

Evening Prayers

Almighty God, I thank You for Your care and protection for the day. I thank You even for the small disappointments and crosses that You have sent me, because I can offer them to You in atonement for my sins and the sins of the world. I thank You for health and safety, for work and recreation, and for rest and quiet now that day is done.

Dear God, I am sorry for the many times today that I must have disappointed You, if not by deliberate sin, at least by neglecting so many opportunities for curbing my tongue, keeping my temper, or helping someone in need. Help me to do better tomorrow and make a little progress every day. Let me never be ungrateful for all You have done for me. Make me always love You more and serve You better.

I love You, dear Jesus; I repent of ever having offended You. Never permit me to offend You again. Grant that I may love You, and then do with me what You will.

O Mary Immaculate, watch over my rest and protect me, waking and sleeping. O all my holy saints who come so often to my aid, I thank you and beg you never to forget me. Holy Guardian Angel, watch over me. Dear Jesus, I commend my soul to You. Amen.

The De Profundis

Out of the depths have I cried unto Thee, O Lord: Lord, hear my voice.

Let Thine ears be attentive to the voice of my supplication.

If Thou, O Lord, wilt mark iniquities: Lord, who shall abide it?

For with Thee there is merciful forgiveness: and by reason of Thy law I have waited for Thee, O Lord.

My soul hath relied on His Word: my soul hath hoped in the Lord.

From the morning watch even until night: let Israel hope in the Lord.

Because with the Lord there is mercy: and with Him is plenteous redemption.

And He shall redeem Israel from all his iniquities.

Eternal rest give to them, O Lord, and let perpetual light shine upon them.

An Offering

O Divine Jesus, lonely tonight in so many tabernacles, without visitor or worshipper, I offer You my lonely heart. May its ever pulsation be a throb of love for You. In Your love, O Jesus, You never sleep. You are never weary of Your vigil for sinners. O lovely Jesus! O lonely Jesus! May my heart be a lamp that burns for You, and You alone. Watch, sacramental Sentinel! Watch for the weary world, for the erring soul, and for Your lonely child. Amen.

JESUS

Gives Himself to His Father for us

(Consecration)

Is given to us by His Father

(Communion)

"I am the bread of life;
whoever comes to me will never hunger,
whoever believes in me will never thirst."
JOHN 6:35

INTRODUCTORY RITES

ENTRANCE SONG

Together we make the Sign of the Cross:

Priest: In the name of the Father, and of the Son, and of the Holy Spirit.

People: **Amen.**

GREETING

The Priest greets us in the name of the Lord:

A Priest: The grace of our Lord Jesus Christ,
and the love of God,
and the communion of the Holy Spirit
be with you all.

Or:

B Priest: Grace to you and peace from God our Father
and the Lord Jesus Christ.

Or:

C Priest: The Lord be with you.

We reply:

People: **And with your spirit.**

THE PENITENTIAL ACT

Priest: Brethren (brothers and sisters), let us
acknowledge our sins,
and so prepare ourselves to celebrate the
sacred mysteries.

A Priest and People:

**I confess to almighty God
and to you, my brothers and sisters,
that I have greatly sinned,
in my thoughts and in my words,
in what I have done and in what I have failed to do,**

We strike our breast:

**through my fault, through my fault,
through my most grievous fault;**

We continue:

**therefore I ask blessed Mary ever-Virgin,
all the Angels and Saints,
and you, my brothers and sisters,
to pray for me to the Lord our God.**

Priest: May almighty God have mercy on us,
forgive us our sins,
and bring us to everlasting life.

People: **Amen.**

Or:

Priest: Brethren (brothers and sisters), let us
acknowledge our sins,
and so prepare ourselves to celebrate the
sacred mysteries.

Priest: Have mercy on us, O Lord.

People: For we have sinned against you.

Priest: Show us, O Lord, your mercy.

People: And grant us your salvation.

At the end of the Act, the Priest prays:

Priest: May almighty God have mercy on us,
forgive us our sins,
and bring us to everlasting life.

People: Amen.

THE KYRIE

*The KYRIE, or "Lord, have mercy," is sung or said
unless it was used in the Penitential Act.*

Priest: Lord, have mercy.

People: Lord, have mercy.

Priest: Christ, have mercy.

People: Christ, have mercy.

Priest: Lord, have mercy.

People: Lord, have mercy.

Or:

Priest: Kyrie, eleison.

People: Kyrie, eleison.

Priest: Christe, eleison.

People: Christe, eleison.

Priest: Kyrie, eleison.

People: Kyrie, eleison.

THE GLORIA

Glory to God in the highest,
and on earth peace to people of good will.
We praise you,
we bless you,
we adore you,
we glorify you,
we give you thanks for your great glory,
Lord God, heavenly King,
O God, almighty Father.

Lord Jesus Christ, Only Begotten Son,
Lord God, Lamb of God, Son of the Father,
you take away the sins of the world,
    have mercy on us;
you take away the sins of the world,
    receive our prayer;
you are seated at the right hand of the Father,
    have mercy on us.

For you alone are the Holy One,
you alone are the Lord,
you alone are the Most High,
Jesus Christ,
with the Holy Spirit,
in the glory of God the Father. Amen.

THE COLLECT

Priest: Let us pray.

We pray silently with the Priest.
He then prays the Collect prayer,
preparing us for the Liturgy of the Word.

He ends the prayer:

Through our Lord Jesus Christ, your Son,
who lives and reigns with you in the unity of the
    Holy Spirit,
one God, for ever and ever.

People: **Amen.**

SIT   LITURGY OF THE WORD

THE FIRST READING

God Speaks to Us through the Old Testament

At the end of the reading:

Lector: The word of the Lord.
People: **Thanks be to God.**

RESPONSORIAL PSALM

The cantor proclaims the psalm, and we respond.

THE SECOND READING

God Speaks to Us through the New Testament

At the end of the reading:

Lector: The word of the Lord.
People: **Thanks be to God.**

GOSPEL ACCLAMATION

*The cantor sings the Alleluia
and we repeat it.*

*During Lent, instead of the Alleluia,
use one of the following or other acclamations:*

A **Praise to you, Lord Jesus Christ, King of
     endless glory!**

B **Praise and honor to you, Lord Jesus Christ!**

C **Glory and praise to you, Lord Jesus Christ!**

D **Glory to you, Word of God, Lord Jesus Christ!**

GOSPEL DIALOGUE

Deacon (or Priest): The Lord be with you.

People: **And with your spirit.**

Deacon (or Priest): A reading from the holy Gospel
              according to N.

People: **Glory to you, O Lord.**

GOSPEL READING

*The Priest or Deacon proclaims
God's Word as we listen.*

At the end of the Gospel:

Deacon (or Priest): The Gospel of the Lord.

People: **Praise to you, Lord Jesus Christ.**

THE HOMILY

STAND   THE PROFESSION OF FAITH

The Nicene Creed

I believe in one God,
the Father almighty,
maker of heaven and earth,
of all things visible and invisible.

I believe in one Lord Jesus Christ,
the Only Begotten Son of God,
born of the Father before all ages.
God from God, Light from Light,
true God from true God,
begotten, not made, consubstantial with the Father;
through him all things were made.
For us men and for our salvation
he came down from heaven,
(All bow during the next three lines)
and by the Holy Spirit was incarnate
    of the Virgin Mary,
and became man.

For our sake he was crucified under Pontius Pilate,
he suffered death and was buried,
and rose again on the third day
in accordance with the Scriptures.

He ascended into heaven
and is seated at the right hand of the Father.
He will come again in glory
to judge the living and the dead
and his kingdom will have no end.

I believe in the Holy Spirit, the Lord, the giver of
     life,
who proceeds from the Father and the Son,
who with the Father and the Son is adored and
     glorified,
who has spoken through the prophets.

I believe in one, holy, catholic and apostolic
     Church.
I confess one Baptism for the forgiveness of sins
and I look forward to the resurrection of the dead
and the life of the world to come. Amen.

PRAYER OF THE FAITHFUL

People: Lord, hear our prayer.

The Priest ends with a prayer:

People: **Amen.**

LITURGY OF THE EUCHARIST

**PRESENTATION AND PREPARATION
OF THE GIFTS**

As the Priest thanks God, we prepare our hearts to
receive the gifts of bread and wine. They will soon
become the Body and Blood of Jesus.

The Priest prays quietly:

Blessed are you, Lord God of all creation,
for through your goodness we have received
the bread we offer you:
fruit of the earth and work of human hands,
it will become for us the bread of life.

People: **Blessed be God for ever.**

*The Priest pours wine and a little water into the chalice,
praying quietly:*

By the mystery of this water and wine
may we come to share in the divinity of Christ,
who humbled himself to share in our humanity.

The Priest raises the chalice slightly, praying quietly:

Blessed are you, Lord God of all creation,
for through your goodness we have received
the wine we offer you:
fruit of the vine and work of human hands,
it will become our spiritual drink.

People: **Blessed be God for ever.**

INVITATION TO PRAYER

Priest: Pray, brethren (brothers and sisters),
that my sacrifice and yours
may be acceptable to God,
the almighty Father.

STAND

People: **May the Lord accept the sacrifice
at your hands
for the praise and glory of his name,
for our good,
and the good of all his holy Church.**

PRAYER OVER THE OFFERINGS

The Priest prays over the offerings. We respond:

People: **Amen.**

EUCHARISTIC PRAYER II
The Preface Dialogue

Priest: The Lord be with you.

People: **And with your spirit.**

Priest: Lift up your hearts.

People: **We lift them up to the Lord.**

Priest: Let us give thanks to the Lord our God.

People: **It is right and just.**

The Preface

We give thanks and praise to God.

It is truly right and just, our duty and our salvation,
always and everywhere to give you thanks, Father
     most holy,
through your beloved Son, Jesus Christ,
your Word through whom you made all things,
whom you sent as our Savior and Redeemer,
incarnate by the Holy Spirit and born of the Virgin.
Fulfilling your will and gaining for you a holy people,
he stretched out his hands as he endured his Passion,
so as to break the bonds of death and manifest the
     resurrection.
And so, with the Angels and all the Saints
we declare your glory,
as with one voice we acclaim:

The Sanctus

Priest and People:

Holy, Holy, Holy Lord God of hosts.
Heaven and earth are full of your glory.
Hosanna in the highest.
Blessed is he who comes in the name of the Lord.
Hosanna in the highest.

KNEEL

Invocation of the Holy Spirit

You are indeed Holy, O Lord,
the fount of all holiness.
Make holy, therefore, these gifts, we pray,
by sending down your Spirit upon them like the
    dewfall,
so that they may become for us
the Body and ✠ Blood of our Lord Jesus Christ.

The Lord's Supper

At the time he was betrayed
and entered willingly into his Passion,
he took bread and, giving thanks, broke it,
and gave it to his disciples, saying:

TAKE THIS, ALL OF YOU, AND EAT OF IT,
FOR THIS IS MY BODY,
WHICH WILL BE GIVEN UP FOR YOU.

In a similar way, when supper was ended,
he took the chalice
and, once more giving thanks,
he gave it to his disciples, saying:

TAKE THIS, ALL OF YOU, AND DRINK FROM IT,
FOR THIS IS THE CHALICE OF MY BLOOD,
THE BLOOD OF THE NEW AND ETERNAL COVENANT,
WHICH WILL BE POURED OUT FOR YOU AND FOR MANY
FOR THE FORGIVENESS OF SINS.

DO THIS IN MEMORY OF ME.

Memorial Acclamation

Priest: The mystery of faith.

People: We proclaim your Death, O Lord,
and profess your Resurrection
until you come again.

Or:

When we eat this Bread and drink this Cup,
we proclaim your Death, O Lord,
until you come again.

Or:

Save us, Savior of the world,
for by your Cross and Resurrection
you have set us free.

Therefore, as we celebrate
the memorial of his Death and Resurrection,
we offer you, Lord,
the Bread of life and the Chalice of salvation,
giving thanks that you have held us worthy
to be in your presence and minister to you.

Humbly we pray
that, partaking of the Body and Blood of Christ,
we may be gathered into one by the Holy Spirit.

Remember, Lord, your Church,
spread throughout the world,
and bring her to the fullness of charity,
together with N. our Pope and N. our Bishop
and all the clergy.

Remember also our brothers and sisters
who have fallen asleep in the hope of the
     resurrection,
and all who have died in your mercy:
welcome them into the light of your face.

Have mercy on us all, we pray,
that with the Blessed Virgin Mary, Mother of God,
with blessed Joseph, her Spouse,
with the blessed Apostles,
and with all the Saints who have pleased you
    throughout the ages,
we may merit to be coheirs to eternal life,
and may praise and glorify you
through your Son, Jesus Christ.

Concluding Doxology

Priest: Through him, and with him, and in him,
        O God, almighty Father,
        in the unity of the Holy Spirit,
        all glory and honor is yours,
        for ever and ever.

People: **Amen.**

Priest: At the Savior's command
           and formed by divine teaching,
           we dare to say:

THE LORD'S PRAYER

Priest and People:

> Our Father, who art in heaven,
> hallowed be thy name;
> thy kingdom come,
> thy will be done
> on earth as it is in heaven.
> Give us this day our daily bread,
> and forgive us our trespasses,
> as we forgive those who trespass against us;
> and lead us not into temptation,
> but deliver us from evil.

Priest: Deliver us, Lord, we pray, from every evil,
           graciously grant peace in our days,
           that, by the help of your mercy,
           we may be always free from sin
           and safe from all distress,
           as we await the blessed hope
           and the coming of our Savior, Jesus Christ.

People: For the kingdom,
           the power and the glory are yours,
           now and for ever.

THE SIGN OF PEACE

The Priest prays for peace, ending with:

Priest: Who live and reign for ever and ever.

People: **Amen.**

Priest: The peace of the Lord be with you always.

People: **And with your spirit.**

We give one another a sign of peace.

THE FRACTION OF THE BREAD

We sing or say:

Lamb of God, you take away the sins of the world,
    have mercy on us.

Lamb of God, you take away the sins of the world,
    have mercy on us.

Lamb of God, you take away the sins of the world,
    grant us peace.

KNEEL   THE PRAYER BEFORE COMMUNION

The Priest prays quietly:

Lord Jesus Christ, Son of the living God,
who, by the will of the Father
and the work of the Holy Spirit,
through your Death gave life to the world,
free me by this, your most holy Body and Blood,
from all my sins and from every evil;
keep me always faithful to your commandments,
and never let me be parted from you.

Or:

May the receiving of your Body and Blood,
Lord Jesus Christ,
not bring me to judgment and condemnation,
but through your loving mercy
be for me protection in mind and body
and a healing remedy.

INVITATION TO COMMUNION

Priest: Behold the Lamb of God,
behold him who takes away the sins of the world.
Blessed are those called to the supper of the Lamb.

Priest and People:

**Lord, I am not worthy
that you should enter under my roof,
but only say the word
and my soul shall be healed.**

The Priest receives the Body and Blood of Christ.

COMMUNION OF THE PEOPLE

Priest: The Body of Christ.
Communicant: Amen.
Priest: The Blood of Christ.
Communicant: Amen.

The Communion Song
We sing the Communion Song together
as we receive Communion.

Period of Silence or Song of Praise
After Communion, we thank God in silent prayer
or a song of praise.

PRAYER AFTER COMMUNION
STAND
Priest: Let us pray.
The Priest prays the Prayer after Communion, ending with:

Priest: Through Christ our Lord.
People: Amen.

CONCLUDING RITES

God has fed us with His Word
and the Body of Christ.
Let us go now to do good works
as we praise and bless the Lord.

THE BLESSING

Priest: The Lord be with you.
People: And with your spirit.
Priest: May almighty God bless you,
the Father, and the Son, ✠ and the Holy Spirit.
People: Amen.

DISMISSAL

Deacon (or Priest):
A   Go forth, the Mass is ended.
B   Go and announce the Gospel of the Lord.
C   Go in peace, glorifying the Lord by your life.
D   Go in peace.
People: Thanks be to God.

Prayers Before Communion

Prayer of Contrition

Dear Jesus, I very much want to receive You in Holy Communion. I am sorry for the ways I have hurt You and others, O Lord, by not doing what is right. Please forgive me!

Most of all, Jesus, thank You for always loving me. By the prayers of Your dear Mother Mary, make me worthy to receive You now.

May this Communion fill me with joy and peace as You come into my heart. Amen.

Act of Offering

Dear Jesus, I offer myself to You this day as I prepare to receive You in Holy Communion. Please make me ready to receive You with all the love in my heart.

Act of Praise

Dear God, I worship You today, Father, Son, and Holy Spirit! Thank You for being my Father and Lover. I praise You for Who You are, Good Shepherd and King of Love. To You be praise, to You be glory, to You be thanksgiving forever and ever! Amen.

Prayers After Communion

O Jesus, You have just come to me in Holy Communion.
Your Body is living in my body.
Your Heart is beating in my heart.

You are truly present in me now.

Thank You so much for coming into my heart!
I am so glad You are here with me.
Please don't ever leave me.
I love You, Jesus.
I want to live forever with You in heaven.

Today I give myself to You.
I give You my body, my mind, my heart.
Please keep me close to Your Heart,
and bring me back to You if ever I stray from You.

Jesus, I love You. Amen.

Anima Christi

Soul of Christ, sanctify me; Body of Christ, save me; Blood of Christ,
inebriate me; Water from the side of Christ, wash me; Passion of
Christ, strengthen me; O good Jesus hear me; Within Your wounds
hide me; Separated from You, let me never be; From the evil one
protect me; At the hour of my death, call me; And close to You bid
me; That with Your saints, I may be, Praising You forever and ever.
Amen.

The Sacrament of Reconciliation

God loves you! He created you because He wants you to live with Him forever. Jesus, God's Son, teaches us to love God with all our hearts, all our minds, and all our souls; and to love our neighbors as ourselves. Sin is our failure to do this; yet God makes a way for us when we fall: the Sacrament of Reconciliation.

Examination of Conscience
(the Ten Commandments)

1. **I am the Lord, Your God. You shall have no other gods before Me.** Do I pray every day? Do I worship God alone? Have I participated in any superstitious practices? Do I let the things of this world (money, prestige, etc.) take precedence over love of God?

2. **You shall not take the name of the Lord in vain.** Do I respect God's name? Do I misuse it out of frustration or anger or to impress those around me? Am I willing to stand up for God?

3. **Remember to keep holy the Lord's day.** Do I celebrate the Eucharist on Sundays and Holy Days? Do I participate, listening closely to the Scripture readings and allowing God to speak to me through them? Do I refrain from work on Sundays except when necessary, and enjoy time with my loved ones when possible?

4. **Honor your Father and Mother.** God puts people in authority to care for, protect, and guide us. Do I obey my superiors and do my tasks willingly? Do I spread peace and happiness or division and unrest? As a parent, do I love and encourage my children? Am I patient with them? Do I spend one-on-one time with them and give them appropriate discipline?

5. **You shall not kill.** God, Who alone gives life, commands us to treat all with care and respect. Do I taunt or fight with others?

Have I injured others through my violence, abuse, or carelessness? Have I abused alcohol or other drugs? Do I forgive readily?

6. **You shall not commit adultery.** *He who finds a wife finds happiness; it is a favor he receives from the LORD.* —PROVERBS 18:22 When two people get married, they promise their mutual love to one another. God wants them to honor that promise and their marriage bond. He calls all of us to be pure and modest in our behavior. Do I respect the dignity of the human body and the holiness of Christian marriage? If married, have I been faithful to my vows? Do I work at building up my marriage? Have I dishonored my body by fornication, impurity or unworthy conversation or thoughts leading to impure actions?

7. **You shall not steal.** Do I respect the property of other people? Have I stolen or damaged what belongs to another? Have I cheated anyone? Have I done my best at work? Am I trustworthy and faithful to my word?

8. **You shall not bear false witness against your neighbor.** Telling the truth, difficult as it may be, helps us live in peace with ourselves and others. Have I lied to protect myself or "get away" with something? Do I gossip about others or hurt their reputation by spreading stories about them?

9. **You shall not covet your neighbor's wife.** *Therefore what God has joined together, no human being must separate.* —MARK 10:9 Have I weakened or damaged my marriage commitment or that of another through my desire for another person? Do I honor my marriage and seek to build up my spouse? Do I respect the commitments of others and help them remain faithful to their promises?

10. **You shall not covet your neighbor's goods.** Am I jealous or envious of the possessions, gifts, and talents of others? Am I grateful for all God has given me, including my life, my abilities, my vocation? Do I share with others?

Prayer Before Confession

Dear God, my Father, You really love me. You understand my weakness and failings. I admit to You today that I have sinned. Please forgive me and give me the strength to walk free of this sin. Thank You for the gift of Reconciliation, a chance to begin again with You. Amen.

How to Go to Confession

- Make the Sign of the Cross as you say, **"Bless me Father, for I have sinned. It has been _____ since my last Confession."**

- Confess your sins.

- When finished, say, **"I am sorry for these and all my sins."**

- The priest will give you a penance, and he may offer you some spiritual direction.

- Pray an Act of Contrition.

Act of Contrition

O my God, I am heartily sorry for having offended You. I detest all my sins because of Your just punishments, but most of all because they offend You, my God, Who are all-good and deserving of all my love. I firmly resolve, with the help of Your grace, to sin no more and to avoid the near occasions of sin. Amen.

Prayers After Confession

Prayer of Saint Odo of Cluny

(879-942)

O only-begotten Son of the sovereign Father, look upon us with a
benign countenance. It is you who called the penitent heart of the
Magdalene to the pinnacle of glory. The lost penny is again restored
to the royal treasury; and the gem wiped clean from mire surpasses
the stars in brilliance. O Jesus, balm on our wounds and sole hope of
the penitent, through the tears of the Magdalene wash away our sins.
O most gracious Mother of God, take us, the weeping descendants of
Eve, from a thousand waves in this life to a haven of safety. To God
alone be glory for His manifold graces — to God who forgives the sins
of sinners and bestows rewards. Amen.

Prayer of Thanksgiving After Confession

Dear God, thank You so much for forgiving me! I feel lighter,
forgiven, renewed, ready to go on with my life. I want to walk in
freedom from sin, to avoid the occasions and places that would lead
me back into it. Lord, I admit I can't do it without You, so please,
through the prayers of Mary, my Mother, help me to continue living
in peace and joy with You and others. In Jesus' name. Amen.

The Stations of the Cross

Based on the Way of the Cross by St Alphonsus Liguori

PREPARATORY PRAYER

My Lord Jesus Christ, You made this journey to die for me with unutterable love, and I have so many times unworthily abandoned You; but now I love You with my whole heart, and because I love You, I repent sincerely for ever having offended You. Pardon me, my God, and permit me to accompany You on this journey. You go to die for love of me; I wish also, my beloved Redeemer, to die for love of You. My Jesus, I will live and die always united to You.

At the beginning of each station:

V.   We adore You, O Christ, and we bless You.

R.   Because by Your holy Cross, You have redeemed the world.

1.   JESUS IS CONDEMNED TO DEATH

Consider how Jesus, after having been scourged and crowned with thorns, was unjustly condemned by Pilate to die on the Cross.

Dear Jesus, it was not Pilate, but my sins that condemned You to die. I ask You, by the merits of this sorrowful journey, to assist my soul in its journey towards eternity. I love You, my beloved Jesus; I repent with my whole heart for having offended You. Never permit me to separate myself from You again. Grant that I may love You always; and then do with me as You will.

Our Father, Hail Mary, Glory be to the Father

At the Cross her station keeping,
Stood the mournful Mother weeping,
Close to Jesus to the last.

42

2. JESUS ACCEPTS HIS CROSS

Consider how Jesus, in making this journey with the Cross on His shoulders, thought of us, and offered to His Father, for us, the death He was about to undergo.

My most beloved Jesus, I embrace all the tribulations You have destined for me until death. I implore You, by the pain You suffered in carrying Your Cross, to give me the necessary help to carry mine with perfect patience and resignation. I love You, Jesus my love; I repent of having offended You. Never permit me to separate myself from You again. Grant that I may love You always; and then do with me as You will.

Our Father, Hail Mary, Glory be to the Father
Through her heart, His sorrow sharing, All His bitter anguish bearing,
Now at length the sword has passed!

3. JESUS FALLS THE FIRST TIME

Consider this first fall of Jesus under His Cross. His flesh was torn by the scourges, His head crowned with thorns, and He had lost a great quantity of blood. He was so weakened that he could scarcely walk, and yet he had to carry this great load upon His shoulders. The soldiers struck Him rudely, and thus He fell several times in His journey.

My beloved Jesus, it is not the weight of the Cross, but my sins, which have made You suffer so much pain. By the merits of this first fall, deliver me from the misfortune of falling into mortal sin. I love You, O my Jesus, with my whole heart; I repent of having offended You. Never permit me to separate myself from You again. Grant that I may love You always; and then do with me as You will.

Our Father, Hail Mary, Glory be to the Father
O, how sad, and sore distressed, Now was she, that Mother Blessed,
of the sole-begotten One.

4. JESUS MEETS HIS SORROWFUL MOTHER

Consider the meeting of the Son and the Mother, which took place on this journey. Jesus and Mary looked at each other, and their looks became as so many arrows to wound those hearts which loved each other so tenderly.

My most loving Jesus, by the sorrow You experienced in this meeting, grant me the grace of a truly devoted love for Your most holy Mother. And you, my Queen, who were overwhelmed with sorrow, obtain for me by your intercession a continual and tender remembrance of the Passion of your Son. I love You, Jesus my love; I repent of ever having offended You. Never permit me to offend You again. Grant that I may love You always; and then do with me as You will.

Our Father, Hail Mary, Glory be to the Father
Woebegone, with heart's prostration, Mother meek, the bitter Passion,
Saw she of her glorious Son.

5. SIMON HELPS JESUS TO CARRY THE CROSS

Consider how the soldiers, seeing that at each step Jesus, from weakness, was on the point of expiring, and fearing that He would die on the way, forced Simon the Cyrenian to carry the Cross behind our Lord.

Dear Jesus, I will not refuse the Cross, as the Cyrenian did; I accept it; I embrace it. I accept in particular the death You have destined for me; with all the pains that may accompany it; I unite it to Your death, I offer it to You. You have died for love of me; I will die for love of You, and to please You. Help me by Your grace. I love You, Jesus my love; I repent of having offended You. Never permit me to offend You again. Grant that I may love You always; and then do with me as You will.

Our Father, Hail Mary, Glory be to the Father
Who could mark, from tears refraining, Christ's dear Mother uncomplaining,
In so great a sorrow bowed?

6. VERONICA WIPES THE FACE OF JESUS

Consider how the holy woman Veronica, seeing Jesus so afflicted, and His face bathed in sweat and blood, presented Him with a towel, with which He wiped His adorable face, leaving on it the impression of His holy countenance.

My most beloved Jesus, Your face was beautiful before, but in this journey it has lost all its beauty, and wounds and blood have disfigured it. Regrettably, my soul also was once beautiful, when it received Your grace in Baptism; but I have disfigured it since by my sins; You alone, my Redeemer, can restore it to its former beauty. Do this by Your Passion, O Jesus. I repent of having offended You. Never permit me to offend You again. Grant that I may love You always; and then do with me as You will.

Our Father, Hail Mary, Glory be to the Father
*Who, unmoved, behold her languish, Underneath His cross of anguish,
'Mid the fierce, unpitying crowd?*

7. JESUS FALLS THE SECOND TIME

Consider the second fall of Jesus under the Cross – a fall which renews the pain of all the wounds of the head and members of our afflicted Lord.

My most gentle Jesus, how many times You have pardoned me, and how many times have I fallen again, and begun again to offend You! By the merits of this new fall, give me the necessary help to persevere in Your grace until death. Grant that in all temptations which beset me I may always commend myself to You. I love You, Jesus my love; I repent of having offended You. Never permit me to offend You again. Grant that I may love You always; and then do with me as You will.

Our Father, Hail Mary, Glory be to the Father
*For His people's sins rejected, She her Jesus, unprotected,
Saw with thorns, with scourges rent.*

8. THE WOMEN OF JERUSALEM WEEP OVER JESUS

Consider how those women wept with compassion at seeing Jesus in such a pitiable state, streaming with blood, as He walked along. But Jesus said to them: "Weep not for Me, but for your children."

My Jesus, laden with sorrows, I weep for the offenses I have committed against You, because of the pains they have deserved, and still more because of the displeasure they have caused You, who have loved me so much. It is Your love, more than the fear of hell, which causes me to weep for my sins. My Jesus, I love You more than myself; I repent of having offended You. Never permit me to offend You again. Grant that I may love You always; and then do with me as You will.

Our Father, Hail Mary, Glory be to the Father
*Saw her Son from judgement taken, Her beloved in death forsaken,
Till His Spirit forth He sent.*

9. JESUS FALLS THE THIRD TIME

Consider the third fall of Jesus Christ. His weakness was extreme, and the cruelty of His executioners was excessive, as they tried to hasten His steps when He had scarcely strength to move.

Oh my outraged Jesus, by the merits of the weakness You suffered in going to Calvary, give me strength sufficient to conquer all human respect, and all my wicked passions, which have led me to despise Your friendship. I love You, Jesus my love, with my whole heart; I repent of having offended You. Never permit me to offend You again. Grant that I may love You always; and then do with me as You will.

Our Father, Hail Mary, Glory be to the Father
*Fount of love and holy sorrow, Mother, may my spirit borrow
Somewhat of your woe profound.*

10. Jesus is Stripped of His Garments

Consider the violence with which the executioners stripped Jesus. His inner garments adhered to His torn flesh, and they dragged them off so roughly that the skin came with them. Comfort your Savior thus cruelly treated, and say to Him:

My innocent Jesus, by the merits of the torments You endured, help me to strip myself of all affection to things of earth, in order that I may place all my love in You, who are so worthy of my love. I love You, O Jesus, with my whole heart; I repent of having offended You. Never permit me to offend You again. Grant that I may love You always; and then do with me as You will.

Our Father, Hail Mary, Glory be to the Father
Unto Christ, with pure emotion, Raise my contrite heart devotion,
Love to read in every wound.

11. Jesus is Nailed to the Cross

Consider how Jesus, after being thrown on the Cross, stretched out His arms, and offered to His eternal Father the sacrifice of His death for our salvation. The executioners nailed His hands and feet, and then, raising the Cross, left Him to die in anguish.

My crucified Jesus, nail my heart to Your Cross, that it may ever remain there, to love You, and never leave You again. I love You more than myself; I repent of having offended You. Never permit me to offend You again. Grant that I may love You always; and then do with me as You will.

Our Father, Hail Mary, Glory be to the Father
Those five wounds on Jesus smitten, Mother! in my heart be written,
Deep as in your own they be.

12. JESUS DIES UPON THE CROSS

Consider how your Jesus, after three hours' Agony on the Cross, consumed at length with anguish, abandons Himself to the weight of His body, bows His head, and dies.

O my dying Jesus, I kiss devoutly the Cross on which You died for love of me. I deserve because of my sins, to die; but Your death is my hope. By the merits of Your death, give me grace to die, embracing Your feet, and burning with love for You. I yield my soul into Your hands. I love You with my whole heart; I repent of ever having offended You. Never permit me to offend You again. Grant that I may love You always; and then do with me as You will.

Our Father, Hail Mary, Glory be to the Father

You, my Savior's Cross who bear, And your Son's rebuke who share, Let me share them both with you.

13. JESUS IS TAKEN DOWN FROM THE CROSS

Consider how, after the death of our Lord, two of His disciples, Joseph and Nicodemus, took Him down from the Cross, and placed Him in the arms of His afflicted Mother, who received Him with unutterable tenderness, and pressed Him to her bosom.

O Mother of Sorrows, for the love of this Son, accept me for your servant, and pray to Him for me. And You, my Redeemer, since You have died for me, permit me to love You; for I desire only You, and nothing more. I love You, my Jesus, and I repent of ever having offended You. Never let me offend You again. Grant that I may love You always; and then do with me as You will.

Our Father, Hail Mary, Glory be to the Father

In the Passion of my Maker, Be my sinful soul partaker, Weep till death, and keep with you.

14. JESUS IS PLACED IN THE TOMB

Consider how the disciples carried the body of Jesus to bury it, accompanied by His holy Mother, who arranged it in the sepulcher with her own hands. They then closed the tomb, and all withdrew.

Oh, my buried Jesus, I kiss the stone that encloses You. But You did rise again the third day. I beseech You, by Your resurrection, make me rise glorious with You at the last day, to be always united with You in heaven, to praise You and love You forever. I love You, and I repent of ever having offended You. Never permit me to offend You again. Grant that I may love You always; and then do with me as You will.

Our Father, Hail Mary, Glory be to the Father
Christ, when You shall call me hence; Be Your Mother my defense;
Be Your Cross my Victory!

15. JESUS RISES FROM THE DEAD!

Consider how, very early on the first day of the week, several women bringing ointment and spices went to the tomb to anoint Jesus' body. When they arrived they found that the stone had been rolled away! Amazed, they entered the empty tomb and saw an angel clothed in white who said to them, "Do not fear! Jesus is not here; he is risen! Behold the place where they laid him."

O Jesus, in the shimmering rays of this morning, a new light dawns on Mary's pierced heart as You resurrect from the dead. Somewhere in the night, You stepped out of the empty grave with the fire of victory in Your Heart and an unconquerable joy in Your Soul as You definitively triumphed over sin and death. Jesus, thank You for living and dying for us, so that we who believe in and follow You will not die, but live in heaven forever with You.

Our Father, Hail Mary, Glory be to the Father
While my body here decays, May my soul Your goodness praise,
Safe in Paradise with You. Amen.

The Rosary

When we pray, we speak to God, vocally or silently, and listen to God in our hearts. He wants us to know Him and love Him. In the Rosary we pray to God with Mary, the Mother of Jesus and our spiritual Mother. As we pray the prayers of the Rosary, we reflect on certain events, or mysteries, in the lives of Jesus and Mary. The Rosary is divided into four groups of five mysteries each. These are the Joyful, Luminous, Sorrowful and Glorious mysteries.

As we consider each mystery of the Rosary, we try to imagine what was happening and what God wants to teach us. We want to get to know Him and to learn how He wants us to live. But even more, to pray the Rosary is to hold Mary's hand and let her bring us to Jesus. When we are with Jesus and Mary, we know the peace, love, and joy of God.

How to Pray the Rosary

- Begin by making the Sign of the Cross and praying the "Apostles' Creed," while you hold the crucifix.
- Pray one "Our Father" on the first bead, three "Hail Marys" on the next three beads for the virtues of Faith, Hope, and Charity, and finish with a "Glory Be to the Father."
- Announce the first Mystery and meditate on it while praying an "Our Father" on the large bead, ten "Hail Marys" on the smaller beads, and finishing with a "Glory Be to the Father." This is one decade.
- If you wish, add the "Fatima Prayer" after the Glory Be:
  "O my Jesus, forgive us our sins; save us from the fires of Hell.
  Lead all souls to Heaven, especially those most in need of Your mercy."

Continue in this way until all you have prayed all five decades. To finish, pray the "Hail Holy Queen."

The Apostles' Creed

I believe in God, the Father almighty,
    Creator of heaven and earth.
    and in Jesus Christ, his only Son, our Lord,
    Who was conceived by the Holy Spirit,
    born of the Virgin Mary,
    suffered under Pontius Pilate,
    was crucified, died, and was buried.

He descended into hell. The third day
    he arose again from the dead.
    He ascended into heaven,
    and is seated at the right hand of God the
    Father Almighty, from whence
    He shall come again to judge the living
    and the dead.

I believe in the Holy Spirit,
    the Holy Catholic Church,
    the communion of saints,
    the forgiveness of sins,
    the resurrection of the body,
    and life everlasting.
    Amen.

Hail, Holy Queen

Hail, holy Queen, Mother of mercy; our life, our sweetness and our hope. To thee do we cry, poor banished children of Eve. To thee do we send up our sighs, mourning and weeping in this valley of tears. Turn then, most gracious Advocate, thine eyes of mercy toward us, and after this our exile show unto us the blessed fruit of thy womb, Jesus. O clement, O loving, O sweet Virgin Mary.

V.   Pray for us, O Holy Mother of God;

R.   **That we made be made worthy of the promises of Christ.**

The Joyful Mysteries

(Monday and Saturday)

THE ANNUNCIATION

In the sixth month, the angel Gabriel was sent from God to a town of Galilee called Nazareth, to a virgin betrothed to a man named Joseph, of the house of David, and the virgin's name was Mary. And coming to her, he said, "Hail, favored one! The Lord is with you." But she was greatly troubled at what was said and pondered what sort of greeting this might be. Then the angel said to her, "Do not be afraid, Mary, for you have found favor with God.

Behold, you will conceive in your womb and bear a son, and you shall name him Jesus."

—LUKE 1:26-31

Just as God called Mary, He is also calling each of us, and giving us abundant grace to respond to Him.

**Dear Mother Mary, through your intercession,
help me say yes to God in all He asks of me, with a willing heart.**

THE VISITATION

During those days Mary set out and traveled to the hill country in haste to a town of Judah, where she entered the house of Zechariah and greeted Elizabeth. When Elizabeth heard Mary's greeting, the infant leaped in her womb, and Elizabeth, filled with the holy Spirit, cried out in a loud voice and said, "Most blessed are you among women, and blessed is the fruit of your womb. And how does this happen to me, that the mother of my Lord should come to me? For at the moment the sound of your greeting reached my ears, the infant in my womb leaped for joy. Blessed are you who believed that what was spoken to you by the Lord would be fulfilled."

—LUKE 1:39-45

Even in the womb Jesus came not to be served, but to serve. Let us also seek to serve others with the love of God.

**Dear Mother Mary, through your intercession,
help me to reach out and care for others with love.**

THE BIRTH OF OUR LORD

While they were there, the time came for her to have her child, and she gave birth to her firstborn son. She wrapped him in swaddling clothes and laid him in a manger, because there was no room for them in the inn.

—LUKE 2:6-7

In the quiet of this Holy Night, God gave His only Son into our hands. The Shepherd came to save his sheep, and the world was forever changed.

**Dear Mother Mary, reveal the love of Your Son Jesus in my heart,
that I may be ever close to Him.**

THE PRESENTATION OF JESUS

*"Now, Master, you may let your servant go
    in peace, according to your word,
for my eyes have seen your salvation,
        which you prepared in sight of all the peoples,
a light for revelation to the Gentiles,
        and glory for your people Israel."*

—LUKE 2:29-32

Let us always believe that God, who fulfilled His promises to Israel His people and Simeon His prophet, will also keep His promises to us His children.

**Dear Mother Mary, help me pray in faith, obey in trust, and wait in hope,
that Our Lord will fulfill all His promises and bring me His salvation.**

THE FINDING OF JESUS

And he said to them, "Why were you looking for me? Did you not know that I must be in my Father's house?" But they did not understand what he said to them.

—LUKE 2:49-50

Jesus' one desire was to always do his Father's Will, no matter what the consequences. May we grow like him in wisdom and grace.

**Dear Mother Mary, help me witness in all my life
to the deep and strong love
God has for me, and to seek Him with all my heart.**

The Luminous Mysteries

(Thursday)

THE BAPTISM OF JESUS IN THE JORDAN

After Jesus was baptized, he came up from the water and behold, the heavens were opened [for him], and he saw the Spirit of God descending like a dove [and] coming upon him. And a voice came from the heavens, saying, "This is my beloved Son, with whom I am well pleased."
—MATTHEW 3:16-17

In this first mystery of light, Jesus receives the Father's love and affirmation even as the Spirit empowers him for the mission only he can fulfill.

Dear Mother Mary, in the Father's embrace Jesus was able to accept and follow His vocation. Help me also receive the Father's love, and do my best to fulfill my mission as well.

THE WEDDING AT CANA

On the third day there was a wedding in Cana in Galilee, and the mother of Jesus was there. When the wine ran short, the mother of Jesus said to him, "They have no wine." [And] Jesus said to her, "Woman, how does your concern affect me? My hour has not yet come." His mother said to the servers, "Do whatever he tells you." Jesus told them, "Fill the jars with water." So they filled them to the brim. Then he told them, "Draw some out now and take it to the headwaiter." So they took it. And when the headwaiter tasted the water that had become wine, without knowing where it came from (although the servers who had drawn the water knew), the headwaiter called the bridegroom and said to him, "Everyone serves good wine first, and then when people have drunk freely, an inferior one; but you have kept the good wine until now."
—JOHN 2:1, 3-5, 7-10

Jesus did this as the first of his signs in Cana in Galilee and so revealed his glory, and his disciples began to believe in him.

Dear Mary, at your request Jesus changed water into wine and opened the hearts of His disciples to faith. Help me also trust in God to turn the water of my life into the wine of His presence.

THE PROCLAMATION OF THE KINGDOM

After John had been arrested, Jesus came to Galilee proclaiming the gospel of God: "This is the time of fulfillment. The kingdom of God is at hand. Repent, and believe in the gospel."
—MARK 1:14-15

"Jesus proclaims the coming of the Kingdom of God, calls to conversion and forgives the sins of all who draw near to him in humble trust."
—POPE JOHN PAUL II

Dear Mother Mary, help me to hear and respond wholeheartedly to the Word of God so powerfully proclaimed by Jesus.

THE TRANSFIGURATION OF JESUS

[Jesus] took Peter, John, and James and went up the mountain to pray. While he was praying his face changed in appearance and his clothing became dazzling white. Then from the cloud came a voice that said, "This is my chosen Son; listen to him."
—LUKE 9:28-29, 35

"The glory of the Godhead shines forth from the face of Christ as the Father commands the astonished Apostles to 'listen to him' and to prepare to experience with him the agony of the Passion, so as to come with him to the joy of the Resurrection and a life transfigured by the Holy Spirit."
—POPE JOHN PAUL II

Dear Mother Mary, help me revere Christ always in my heart.

THE INSTITUTION OF THE EUCHARIST

When the hour came, he...took the bread, said the blessing, broke it, and gave it to them, saying, "This is my body, which will be given for you; do this in memory of me." And likewise the cup after they had eaten, saying, "This cup is the new covenant in my blood, which will be shed for you."
—LUKE 22:14, 19-20

"A final mystery of light is the institution of the Eucharist, in which Christ...testifies 'to the end' his love for humanity, for whose salvation he will offer himself in sacrifice."
—POPE JOHN PAUL II

Dear Mother Mary, may I always be grateful for this precious gift.

The Sorrowful Mysteries

(Tuesday, Friday)

THE AGONY IN THE GARDEN

Then they came to a place named Gethsemane, and he said to his disciples, "Sit here while I pray." He took with him Peter, James, and John, and began to be troubled and distressed. Then he said to them, "My soul is sorrowful even to death. Remain here and keep watch." He advanced a little and fell to the ground and prayed that if it were possible the hour might pass by him; he said, "Abba, Father, all things are possible to you. Take this cup away from me, but not what I will but what you will."

—MARK 14:32-36

Jesus stayed awake, suffering for us. Can we not stay awake, on our guard against sin? The Spirit will protect us if we abide in Him.

Dear Mother Mary, please pray with me for the grace to accept the sufferings and struggles of my life, in union with Jesus, trusting that God has a plan for me and is able to work it all out for the good. Through your intercession, may God give me the grace to overcome temptation, for His sake.

THE SCOURGING AT THE PILLAR

Pilate again said to them in reply, "Then what [do you want] me to do with [the man you call] the king of the Jews?" They shouted again, "Crucify him." So Pilate, wishing to satisfy the crowd, released Barabbas to them and, after he had Jesus scourged, handed him over to be crucified.

—MARK 15:12-13, 15

Our salvation was purchased, not with glory and fame, but with Jesus' suffering and rejection. Let us remember this when we are tempted to sin or to seek approval from others.

Dear Mother Mary, may I seek to love rather than be loved, and to shine the warmth of Jesus on all I meet.

THE CROWNING WITH THORNS

There was in him no stately bearing to make us look at him,
nor appearance that would attract us to him.
He was spurned and avoided by men,
a man of suffering, accustomed to infirmity,
One of those from whom men hide their faces,
spurned, and we held him in no esteem.
—ISAIAH 53:2-3

Jesus courageously and silently endured this public humiliation, all the while loving and forgiving His aggressors.

Dear Mother Mary, help me remember Jesus in his humility,
especially when I face opposition for speaking the truth.

JESUS CARRIES THE CROSS

But what credit is there if you are patient when beaten for
doing wrong? But if you are patient when you suffer for doing
what is good, this is a grace before God. For to this you have
been called, because Christ also suffered for you, leaving you an
example that you should follow in his footsteps.
—1 PETER 2:20-21

On His way to Calvary, Jesus endured hate, rage, and disgust. Saddened but resolute, He kept on, toward His final end.

Dear Mother Mary, help me accept the crosses God chooses for me,
remembering Jesus will never leave me nor forsake me.

JESUS DIES ON THE CROSS

My God, my God, why have you abandoned me?
Why so far from my call for help,
from my cries of anguish?
My God, I call by day, but you do not answer;
by night, but I have no relief.
In you our ancestors trusted;
they trusted and you rescued them.
—PSALM 22:2-3, 5

Thus the Good Shepherd lays down his life for His sheep. By His suffering and death, Jesus opens the gates of heaven and wins for us all a new life.

Dear Mother Mary, please grant to all humanity the grace of repentance,
conversion, and final homecoming to the Father's House.

The Glorious Mysteries

(Sunday, Wednesday)

THE RESURRECTION

When the sabbath was over, Mary Magdalene, Mary, the mother of James, and Salome bought spices so that they might go and anoint him. On entering the tomb they saw a young man sitting on the right side, clothed in a white robe, and they were utterly amazed. He said to them, "Do not be amazed! You seek Jesus of Nazareth, the crucified. He has been raised; he is not here. Behold the place where they laid him. But go and tell his disciples and Peter, 'He is going before you to Galilee; there you will see him, as he told you.'"

—MARK 16:1, 5-7

Somewhere in the night, the Crucified One stepped out of the tomb with the fire of victory in His Heart and an unconquerable joy in His Soul. After unutterable suffering, mockery, and death, Jesus triumphed! What's more, He did it for us, so we could share in His absolute victory over sin and death. Alleluia!

Dear Mother Mary, please intercede with me for the grace of a strong and vibrant faith in the God who has won my redemption!

THE ASCENSION

Then he led them [out] as far as Bethany, raised his hands, and blessed them. As he blessed them he parted from them and was taken up to heaven.

—LUKE 24:50-51

Ever the Good Shepherd, Jesus gives His disciples a final blessing, imparting to them peace, grace and strength to carry out His mission and bring His Kingdom to the whole world.

Dear Mother Mary, you were there when your Son came into the world and when He left it. Help us to know His abiding presence and peace as we seek to be Christ to others.

THE DESCENT OF THE HOLY SPIRIT

*For you did not receive a spirit of slavery to fall back into fear,
but you received a spirit of adoption, through which we cry,
Abba, "Father!"*

—ROMANS 8:15

God keeps His Word! His promised Spirit now fills the
apostles and the whole Church. Filled with power, we are
freed to do good.

**Dear Mother Mary, please pray for the Spirit to anoint me with the fire of God's
love and the truth of His Word to bring His Kingdom to all.**

THE ASSUMPTION OF MARY

*"May God make this redound to your everlasting honor,
rewarding you with blessings, because you risked your life when
your people were being oppressed, and you averted our disaster,
walking uprightly before our God." And all the people
answered, "Amen! Amen!"*

—JUDITH 13:20

Through the gift of God and her obedience, Mary was
ever preserved free from sin. In His great love and honor
for her who had stood faithfully by Him through it all, Jesus took His Mother,
body and soul, to heaven with Him, forever.

**Dear Mother Mary, in your obedient faithfulness, you triumphed completely over
the Enemy and were exalted by the Most High. Help me also be faithful to God's
Will that I may someday reign in heaven with you.**

THE CORONATION OF MARY

And Mary said:
*"My soul proclaims the greatness of the Lord;
   my spirit rejoices in God my savior.
For he has looked upon his handmaid's lowliness;
   behold, from now on will all ages call me blessed.
The Mighty One has done great things for me,
   and holy is his name."*

—LUKE 1:46-49

God promised, Mary responded. God invited, Mary accepted. God exalted,
Mary rejoiced.

**Dear Mother Mary, behold your children! Wrap us in your mantle of love that we
may always proclaim the greatness of the Lord and rejoice in His salvation.
He loves us! Amen!**

59

Prayer to Our Lady of Guadalupe for Hope & Strength

O Immaculate and Perpetual Virgin of Guadalupe, you appeared on Mount Tepeyac to reconcile all people to God. You told Saint Juan Diego, "I am your mother. Are you not under my protection? Why do you fear, if you are in my mantle, and in my arms?" You left your image on his tilma, using a humble vessel to bring God's grace into the world. Your love gave Saint Juan Diego the courage and strength he needed to face a skeptical bishop and bring about the conversion of his nation. Because of his faithfulness, the Gospel of Our Lord spread through your image, and many people came to believe in Christ.

Dear Lady of Guadalupe, on Tepeyac you proclaimed yourself our Mother and Protectress. Your devotion lives on in the people of Mexico, the Americas, and the whole world. Obtain for us from your most holy Son the grace of keeping our faith, hope in the midst of the trials of life, love for all people, and the precious gift of final perseverance. Amen.

Prayer Before A Crucifix

Look down upon me,
good and gentle Jesus,
while before Your face
I humbly kneel and with
burning soul pray
and beseech You
to fix deep in my heart
lively sentiments of faith,
hope, and charity;
true contrition for my sins, and a
firm purpose of amendment;

While I contemplate, with great love and tender pity, Your five most precious wounds, pondering over them within me and calling to mind the words which David, Your prophet, said of You, my Jesus:

"They have pierced my hands and my feet,
They numbered all my bones."

Amen.

Favorite Catholic Prayers

The Angelus

V. The Angel of the Lord declared unto Mary.
R. **And she conceived by the Holy Spirit.**
(Hail Mary....)
V. Behold the handmaid of the Lord.
R. **Be it done unto me according to thy word.**
(Hail Mary....)
V. And the Word was made Flesh.
R. **And dwelt among us.**
(Hail Mary....)
V. Pray for us, O Holy Mother of God.
R. **That we may be made worthy of the promises of Christ.**

Let us pray: Pour forth, we beseech Thee, O Lord, Thy grace into our hearts; that we to whom the Incarnation of Christ, Thy Son, was made known by the message of an Angel, may by His Passion and Cross, be brought to the glory of His Resurrection. Through the same Christ our Lord. Amen.

Memorare

Remember, O most gracious Virgin Mary, that never was it known, that any one who fled to thy protection, implored thy help or sought thy intercession, was left unaided. Inspired by this confidence, I fly unto thee, O Virgin of virgins, my Mother. To thee do I come, before thee I stand, sinful and sorrowful; O Mother of the Word Incarnate, despise not my petitions, but in thy mercy hear and answer me. Amen.

Prayer to the Holy Spirit

Come, Holy Spirit, fill the hearts of Your faithful,
and kindle in them the fire of Your love.
V.   Send forth Your Spirit and we shall be created.
R.   **And You shall renew the face of the earth.**

Let us pray: O God, Who has instructed the hearts of
Your faithful by the light of the Holy Spirit, grant us,
in the same Spirit, to be truly wise, and ever to rejoice
in His consolation. Through Christ our Lord. Amen.

Grace Before Meals

Bless us, O Lord, and these Thy gifts, which we are about to receive
from Thy bounty, through Christ our Lord. Amen.

Grace After Meals

We give Thee thanks, O Lord, for these and all the blessings which
we have received from Thy bounty, through Christ our Lord. Amen.

Anima Christi

Soul of Christ, sanctify me; Body of Christ, save me;

Blood of Christ, inebriate me;

Water from the side of Christ, wash me;

Passion of Christ, strengthen me; O good Jesus hear me;

Within Your wounds hide me; Separated from You, let me never be;

From the evil one protect me; At the hour of my death, call me;

And close to You bid me; That with Your saints, I may be,

Praising You forever and ever. Amen.

Prayer to Our Lady of Mt. Carmel

O Most beautiful Flower of Mount Carmel, Fruitful Vine, Splendour of Heaven, Blessed Mother of the Son of God, Immaculate Virgin, assist me in this my necessity. O Star of the Sea, help me and show me herein you are my Mother.

O Holy Mary, Mother of God, Queen of Heaven and Earth, I humbly beseech you from the bottom of my heart, to help me in this necessity; there are none that can withstand your power. O, show me herein you are my Mother.

Saint Simon Stock receives the Scapular from Our Lady of Mt. Carmel

O Mary, conceived without sin, pray for us who have recourse to thee. *(three times)*

Sweet Mother, I place this cause in your hands. *(three times)*

The Brown Scapular

What is the Brown Scapular?

The Brown Scapular consists of two small pieces of cloth, connected by two long cords worn over the head and resting on the shoulders.

The History of the Brown Scapular

According to tradition, over 700 years ago Our Blessed Mother appeared to Saint Simon Stock, holding out to him a brown woolen scapular. *"Receive My beloved son, the Scapular of thy Order, as a distinctive sign of My Confraternity. Whoever dies invested with this Scapular shall be preserved from the eternal flames. It is a sign of salvation, a sure safeguard in danger, a pledge of peace and of My special protection until the end of the ages."* The Scapular, then, is a special garment worn as a sign of love and devotion to Mary our Mother and Queen.

What are the conditions of wearing a Brown Scapular?

- Wear the Brown Scapular continuously.
- Observe chastity according to one's state in life (married/single).
- Pray daily the "Little Office of the Blessed Virgin Mary."
  You may substitute any of the following:
  - To observe the fasts of the Church
  - To pray five decades of the Holy Rosary
  - or with the permission of a priest to do a good work.

Pope John Paul II wrote: *"I too have worn the Scapular of Carmel over my heart for a long time!...The most genuine form of devotion to the Blessed Virgin, expressed by the humble sign of the Scapular, is consecration to her Immaculate Heart."*

To wear the Brown Scapular is to trust in Our Lady who has great power of intercession before her Son. It is always a powerful means of grace because it always assures us of Mary's continuous prayers.

Pope Benedict XV, the celebrated World War I Pontiff, granted 500 days' indulgence for devoutly kissing your Scapular. Indulgence is the remission in whole or in part for the temporal punishment (time spent in Purgatory) due to sins.

Benediction of the Blessed Sacrament

The heart of the Eucharist is its celebration in liturgy and its reception in Holy Communion. According to Vatican II, all legitimate devotions such as Exposition, Benediction, Adoration, etc., springing from the Eucharist must flow from the celebration and lead to the reception of Holy Communion.

Benediction of the Blessed Sacrament is a blessing with the monstrance following some time of prayer and devotion before Our Lord present in the Blessed Sacrament. Adoration, or prayer before the Blessed Sacrament, includes the attitudes of adoration, thanksgiving, contrition, and petition. As such it is an extension of the spirit of prayer which should fill the heart of Christians during liturgy.

Adoration also prepares us for reception of Holy Communion by deepening our union with Christ in the Holy Spirit. An intimate union with Christ flows from such prayer.

Early in his pontificate, Pope John Paul II himself opened a chapel of Perpetual Eucharistic Adoration at Saint Peter's Basilica, signaling his great desire that the faithful renew their love for Eucharistic devotion. By his teaching, travels, and example, the Holy Father promoted worldwide resurgence of such devotion.

"The worship given to the Trinity of the Father and of the Son and of the Holy Spirit...must fill our churches...Adoration of Christ in this sacrament of love must also find expression in various forms of Eucharistic devotion: personal prayer before the Blessed Sacrament, hours of adoration, periods of exposition...Eucharistic benediction...Let us be generous with our time in going to meet him...in contemplation that is full of faith and ready to make reparation for the great faults and crimes of the world. May our adoration never cease."

—POPE JOHN PAUL II

The Divine Praises

Blessed be God.

Blessed be His Holy Name.

Blessed be Jesus Christ, true God and true man.

Blessed be the name of Jesus.

Blessed be His Most Sacred Heart.

Blessed be His Most Precious Blood.

Blessed be Jesus in the Most Holy Sacrament of the Altar.

Blessed be the Holy Spirit, the Paraclete.

Blessed be the great Mother of God, Mary most holy.

Blessed be her holy and Immaculate Conception.

Blessed be her glorious Assumption.

Blessed be the name of Mary, Virgin and Mother.

Blessed be Saint Joseph, her most chaste spouse.

Blessed be God in His Angels and in His Saints.

May the heart of Jesus,
in the Most Blessed Sacrament,
be praised, adored, and loved
with grateful affection, at every moment,
in all the tabernacles of the world,
even to the end of time. Amen.

O Salutaris Hostia / O Saving Victim

O Salutaris Hostia

Quae coeli pandis ostium.

Bella premunt hostilia;

Da robur, fer auxilium.

Uni trinoque Domino

Sit sempiterna gloria:

Qui vitam sine termino,

Nobis donet in patria.

Amen.

–Latin text: Saint Thomas Aquinas

O Saving Victim opening wide

The gate of heaven to all below.

Our foes press on from every side;

Thine aid supply, Thy strength bestow.

To Thy great name be endless praise

Immortal Godhead, One in Three;

Oh, grant us endless length of days,

In our true native land with Thee.

Amen.

–English text: Edward Caswall

Tantum Ergo / Down in Adoration Falling

Tantum ergo sacramentum
Veneremur cernui:
Et antiquum documentum
Novo cedat ritui:
Praestet fides supplementum
Sensuum defectui.

Genitori, genitoque
Laus et iubilatio,
Salus, honor virtus quoque
Sit et benedictio:
Procedenti ab utroque
Compar sit laudatio. Amen.

–LATIN TEXT: SAINT THOMAS AQUINAS

Down in adoration falling,
This great Sacrament we hail;
Over ancient forms of worship
Newer rites of grace prevail;
Faith will tell us Christ is present,
When our human senses fail.

To the everlasting Father,
And the Son who made us free,
And the Spirit, God proceeding
From them each eternally,
Be salvation, honor, blessing,
Might and endless majesty. Amen.

–ENGLISH TEXT: EDWARD CASWALL

Adoration of the Blessed Sacrament

Opening Prayer to the Blessed Sacrament

My Lord Jesus Christ, is is Your great love for us that keeps You day and night in this Sacrament, full of pity and love, expecting, inviting, and welcoming all who visit You. I believe that You are really present in the Sacrament of the Altar. From the depth of my nothingness, I adore You; and I thank You for the many graces You have given me, especially for the gift of Yourself in this Sacrament, for the gift of Your most holy Mother as my intercessor, and for the privilege of visiting You in this church.

I now speak to Your most loving Heart with a threefold intention: to thank You for the gift of Yourself; to atone for all the insults which Your enemies heap upon You in this Sacrament; and to adore You wherever Your Eucharistic Presence is dishonored or forgotten.

My Jesus, I love You with my whole heart. I am very sorry for my ingratitude to Your infinite goodness. I now resolve, with the help of Your grace, never to offend You again. And, sinful as I am, I consecrate to You my entire self, my whole will, my affections, my desires, and all that I have. From now on, do with me and mine as You please. I ask for and desire only Your love, final perseverance, and the grace always to do Your Holy Will.

I intercede with You for the souls in purgatory, especially for those who were most devoted to the Blessed Sacrament, and to Your most holy Mother. I recommend to You also, all poor sinners. And lastly, my dear Savior, I unite all my desires with the desires of Your most loving Heart. Thus united, I present them to Your Eternal Father and beg Him in Your Name and for the love of You to hear and answer them. Amen.

—Saint Alphonsus Liguori

Closing Prayer to the Blessed Sacrament

As this time of Love closes, Oh Jesus, I renew my faith and trust in You. I am refreshed after all these hours with You and I count myself among a privileged number, even as Your disciples were, who shared Your actual presence.

Realizing that my visit to You is of little avail unless I try to live a better life and set a better example, I am resolved to go forth again to my duties and concerns with a renewed spirit of perseverance and good will. In my daily life I will try to love and serve God well, and love my neighbor also, for those two things go together. I will try to be a true disciple, indeed. Help me, Oh Jesus, in this my resolution.

Bless me, dear Lord, before I go. And bless not me alone, O Lord, but all as well who are here present, and all who could not come, especially the sick and the dying. Bless our homes and everyone there. Bless all our lives and the hour of our death.

Grant rest to the souls of the faithful departed, and bring them into the light of Your divine glory. So may we who have worshipped You and have been blessed by You here on earth come to behold the radiant glory of Your unveiled countenance in heaven forever and ever. Amen.

The Last Prayer

O, Sweet Jesus, let me lay at Your sacred feet my daily share of joys, struggles, and sorrows, of hopes, fears, and failings. Gather them tenderly into Your most Sacred Heart. Solace my doubts and calm my fears. Grant that I may become more united to You. Amen.

Act of Consecration to the Most Sacred Heart of Jesus

Pray every day for nine days

O most loving Jesus, Redeemer of the human race, behold us humbly prostrate before Your altar. We are Yours and Yours we wish to be. But to be more surely united to You, behold each one of us freely consecrates himself today to Your most Sacred Heart. Many, indeed, have never known You; many, too, despising Your precepts, have rejected You. Have mercy on them all, most merciful Jesus, and draw them to Your Sacred Heart.

Be King, O Lord, not only of the faithful who have never forsaken You, but also of the prodigal children who have abandoned You. Grant that they may quickly return to their Father's house, lest they die of wretchedness and hunger.

Be King of all those who are still involved in the darkness of idolatry whom discord keeps aloof, and call them back to the harbor of truth and unity of faith, so that soon there may be but one flock and one Shepherd.

Grant, O Lord, to Your Church, assurance of freedom and immunity from harm. Give peace and order to all nations. Make the earth resound from pole to pole with one cry, "Praise to the divine Heart that wrought our salvation. To it be glory and honor forever." Amen.

Novena to
Our Lady of the
Miraculous Medal

O Immaculate Virgin Mary,
Mother of Our Lord Jesus and
our Mother, penetrated with the
most lively confidence in your all-
powerful and never-failing
intercession, manifested so often
through the Miraculous Medal,
we your loving and trustful
children implore you to obtain
for us the graces and favor we ask
during this novena, if they be beneficial to our immortal souls,
and the souls for whom we pray. *(Here make your petition.)*

You know, O Mary, how often our souls have been the
sanctuaries of your Son who hates iniquity. Obtain for us then
a deep hatred of sin and that purity of heart which will attach
us to God alone so that our every thought, word and deed may
tend to His greater glory. Obtain for us also a spirit of prayer
and self-denial that we may recover by penance what we have
lost by sin and at length attain to that Blessed Abode where
you reign as the Queen of Angels. Amen.

Novena Prayer to Saint Joseph

This prayer is over 1900 years old. Pray it for nine consecutive mornings for anything you may desire. It has rarely been known to fail.

O Saint Joseph whose protection is so great, so strong, so prompt before the Throne of God, I place in you all my interests and desires.

O Saint Joseph, do assist me by your powerful intercession and obtain for me from your Divine Son all spiritual blessings through Jesus Christ, Our Lord; so that having engaged here below your Heavenly power I may offer my Thanksgiving and Homage to the most Loving of Fathers.

O Saint Joseph, I never weary contemplating you and Jesus asleep in your arms. I dare not approach while He reposes near your heart. Press Him in my name and kiss His fine Head for me, and ask Him to return the Kiss when I draw my dying breath. Saint Joseph, Patron of departing souls, pray for us. Amen.

This prayer was found in the fiftieth year of Our Lord Jesus Christ. In the 1500's it was sent by the Pope to Emperor Charles when he was going into battle.

Whoever reads this prayer, hears it or carries it, will never die a sudden death, nor be drowned, nor will poison take effect on them. They will not fall into the hands of the enemy nor be burned in any fire, nor will they be defeated in battle.

Novena to Saint Jude for Courage

Patron Saint of Difficult Cases

Saint Jude, glorious apostle, faithful servant and friend of Jesus, I come to you this day. As a young man, you left everything to follow Jesus. Your mother, Mary of Cleopas, had the courage to stand beneath the Cross of Christ when so many abandoned Him. You yourself are pictured bearing on your chest His image, with which you cured and converted a pagan ruler of the Middle East. You paid the ultimate price for your faith, suffering martyrdom in Persia.

Saint Jude, you enjoy a worldwide reputation of coming quickly to the aid of all in need, especially those in difficult or desperate situations. Please pray that God will give me courage and strength to do all He asks of me this day. I especially ask your help in this my need (*here mention your request*).

Dear Saint Jude, please help me to 'cast all my cares on the Lord, for He cares for me.' Thank you for the help you are even now bringing to me. Truly I can do all things through Christ who strengthens me. In Jesus' name I pray, Amen.

"To the one who is able to keep you from stumbling and to present you unblemished and exultant, in the presence of his glory, to the only God, our savior, through Jesus Christ our Lord be glory, majesty, power, and authority from ages past, now, and for ages to come. Amen."

—Jude 24-25

The Chaplet of The Divine Mercy

Jesus I Trust In You!

*For private recitation
on ordinary rosary beads*

Our Father...,
Hail Mary...,
the Apostles' Creed.

*Then, on the Our Father beads you
will say the following words:*

Eternal Father, I offer You the
Body and Blood, Soul and
Divinity of Your dearly beloved Son, Our Lord Jesus Christ, in
atonement for our sins and those of the whole world.

On the Hail Mary beads you will say the following words:

For the sake of His sorrowful Passion, have mercy on us and on
the whole world.

In conclusion three times you will recite these words:

Holy God, Holy Mighty One, Holy Immortal One, have mercy
on us and on the whole world.

"The Chaplet of The Divine Mercy" is excerpted from *Divine Mercy in My Soul: The Diary of Saint Faustina M. Kowalska,* copyright 1987, printed with permission of the Marian Fathers of the Immaculate Conception, Stockbridge, MA 01263.

Novena to
Our Lady
of Perpetual Help

See at your feet, O Mother of Perpetual Help, a poor sinner who has recourse to you and confides in you. O Mother of Mercy, have pity on me! I hear you called the refuge and the hope of sinners; be my refuge and my hope.

Help me, for the love of Jesus Christ; stretch forth your hand to a poor fallen sinner. I entrust myself to your tender care and ask that you remember my needs. *(Here mention your request.)*

I bless and thank Almighty God, who in His mercy has given me this confidence in you, a sure pledge of eternal salvation.

Mother of Perpetual Help, grant that we may be delivered through the help of your intercession, from the slavery of all our sins. Amen.

Prayers for Healing

Ancient Prayer to the Virgin Mary

We turn to you for protection, holy Mother of God.
Listen to our prayers, and help us in our needs.
Save us from every danger, glorious and blessed Virgin.

Prayer for Healing

O Heavenly Father, God of Love, You gave us Your Son Jesus to be not only Physician of our souls but Healer of our bodies and minds as well. Lord Jesus, I turn to You in this time of illness. Please come to me now, and lay Your healing hands on me. Let the warmth, peace and healing power of Your Spirit fill me now with Your life and love. I receive You, Lord Jesus!

Heal me according to Your Divine Will, Lord Jesus, and enable me to serve You with a healthy body, soul, and spirit. May Your Joy, O Lord, be my strength this day. Amen.

Healing Prayer for Others

Based on the prayer of a 7th Century Irish Monk

Heavenly Father, Creator of the universe, and Author of its laws, you can bring the dead back to life, and heal those who are sick. We pray for our sick brothers and sisters that they may feel Your hand upon them, renewing their bodies and refreshing their souls. Show to them the affection in which You hold all Your creatures, and grant them an early recovery, in Jesus Name. Amen.

"Pray, hope, and don't worry!"
—Saint Pio of Pietrelcina

Prayer for a Sick Person

Most merciful Jesus, You are the consolation and salvation of all who put their trust in You. We humbly implore You, by Your most bitter passion, grant the recovery of health to Your servant *(name)* according to Your Divine Will, that together we might praise and magnify Your holy Name. Fill them with Your light and Your love, and grant them consolation in their hour of illness. We ask all this through the merits of Your passion, death, and Resurrection. Amen.

Our Father, Hail Mary, Glory Be to the Father.

A Prayer in Sickness

O Lord Jesus Christ, Healer of our souls and bodies, may Your presence be ever with me to make holy and bless this my sickness to Your praise and glory, and to the salvation of my soul. Forgive me all my sins and the times I have not loved You. Help me fix my thoughts upon Your great suffering upon the Cross, that I may learn from You courage and patience, humility and love; and above all, true submission to the Father's Will. May I, being restored to health in Your own good time, show forth Your praise by giving up myself to Your service. Finally, grant that when this life is ended I may be found worthy through Your merit to inherit eternal life. Amen.

The Anointing of the Sick

The Anointing of the Sick is a sacrament that gives a special grace to those facing serious illness or old age. This sacrament originates from the epistle of Saint James, where he exhorts those who are sick to summon the presbyters who are to pray over and anoint the sick with oil in the Lord's name. Saint James declares that the prayer of faith will save the sick person, the person's sins will be forgiven, and the Lord will raise him up.

Each time a Christian falls seriously ill, he or she may receive the Anointing of the Sick, and again if the illness worsens. A priest typically administers this sacrament, using blessed oil. The effects of this sacrament are:

- the uniting of the sick person to the passion of Christ, for their own good and that of the whole Church;
- the strengthening, peace, and courage to endure in a Christian manner the sufferings of illness or old age;
- the forgiveness of sins;
- the restoration of health, if it is conducive to the salvation of their soul;
- the preparation for passing over to eternal life.

Prayer for a Happy Death

O my Lord and Savior, support me in my last hour by the strong arms of Thy sacraments, and the fragrance of Thy consolations. Let Thy absolving words be said over me, and the holy oil sign and seal me; and let Thy own Body be my food, and Thy Blood my sprinkling; and let Thy Mother Mary come to me, and my angel whisper peace to me, and Thy glorious saints and my own dear patrons smile on me, that in and through them all I may die as I desire to live, in Thy Church, in Thy faith, and in Thy love. Amen. My Jesus, mercy.

—Cardinal Newman

Prayer for the Dying

Most Merciful Jesus, lover of souls, I pray to You, by the agony of Your most Sacred Heart, and by the sorrows of Your Immaculate Mother, to wash in Your Most Precious Blood, all those who are now in their agony, and who will die today. I commit them to Your Divine Mercy, to the heart of Our Blessed Mother, and to the care of Saint Joseph, Patron of a happy death. May the angels lead them into paradise, may the saints come to greet them, and with Lazarus, who once was dead, may they have everlasting life. Amen. Sacred Heart of Jesus, I put my trust in You. Jesus, Mary, and Joseph, I love you; save souls.

Prayer for the Faithful Departed

O God, You are filled with mercy and compassion. We beseech You on behalf of the souls of Your servants whom You have called out of this world: look upon them with pity and let them be conducted by the holy angels to paradise, their true country. Grant that they who believed in You and hoped in You may not be left to suffer the pain of punishment, but may be admitted to eternal joy. Through Jesus Christ, Your Son our Lord, Who with You and the Holy Spirit lives and reigns world without end. Amen.

Our Father, Hail Mary, Glory Be to the Father.

Eternal Rest

Eternal rest grant unto them, O Lord, and let perpetual light shine upon them. May they rest in peace. Amen.

O Lord hear my prayer, and let my cry come to you.

O God, the Creator and Redeemer of all the faithful, grant to the souls of your departed servants the remission of all their sins, that through our prayers they may obtain that pardon which they have always desired. Amen.

Prayer for the Holy Father

God, our Father, we ask You to look with mercy and love on Your servant, (name) whom You have chosen to govern Your Church and shepherd Your people. May he, through word and through example, direct, sustain and encourage the people in his care so that with them he may share everlasting life in Your Kingdom. Amen.

May the Lord preserve our Holy Father, (name). May He give him life and protect him in this life and reserve for him the reward of the just. Amen.

My Daily Prayer for Priests

O almighty eternal God, look upon the face of Your Son, and for the love of Him who is the eternal High Priest, have pity on your priests. Stir up in them the grace of their vocation which is in them by the imposition of the bishop's hands. Keep them close to You, lest the enemy prevail against them, so that they may never do anything in the slightest degree unworthy of their sublime vocation.

O Jesus, I pray for Your faithful and fervent priests, for Your unfaithful and tepid priests, for Your priests laboring at home, or abroad in distant mission fields, for Your tempted priests, for Your lonely and desolate priests, for Your young priests, for Your aged priests, for Your sick priests, for Your dying priests, for the souls of Your priests in purgatory.

But above all I commend to You the priests dearest to me: the priest who baptized me, the priests who absolved me from my sins, the priests whose Masses I attended and who gave me Your Body and Blood in Holy Communion, the priests who taught me and instructed me or helped me and encouraged me, and all the priests to whom I am indebted in any other way, particularly _____.

O Jesus, keep them all close to Your heart, and bless them abundantly in time and in eternity. Amen.

Prayers for the Poor

Mother Teresa's Prayer for the Poor

Make us worthy, Lord, to serve our brothers and sisters throughout the world who live and die in poverty and hunger. Give them through our hands this day their daily bread, and by our understanding love give them peace and joy. Amen.

Oh God...We adore You, we love You with our whole heart and soul...We desire to love You on earth as the blessed do in heaven.

We adore all the designs of Your divine Providence, and surrender ourselves entirely to Your Will. We also love our neighbors for Your sake, just as much as we love ourselves.

We sincerely forgive all who have injured us and ask pardon of all whom we have injured. Amen.

Prayer for the Unemployed

Dear Heavenly Father, You promise to provide for all of our needs according to your glorious riches in Christ Jesus. We pray for all who find themselves unemployed or under-employed at this time. Grant them courage, patience, and faith that they will soon find meaningful and satisfying work, according to Your Will.

Please guide and direct their paths, and restore their hope and self-esteem. Help them provide for their needs and those of their families. Most of all, may they know for themselves Your faithful and compassionate love, a love that will see them through this and all the difficulties of this life, and bring them to everlasting life with You. Amen.

Family Prayers

Family Prayer

God made us a family.
We need one another.
We love one another.
We forgive one another.
We work together.
We play together.
We worship together.
Together we learn God's Word.
Together we grow in Christ.
Together we love all people.
Together we serve our God.
Together we hope for Heaven.
These are our hopes.
Help us to obtain them, Father,
through Jesus Your Son, Our Lord. Amen.

Prayer for Parents

Dear Heavenly Father, thank You for the gift of parents, who bring life into this world. Through the intercession of Our Blessed Mother Mary and good Saint Joseph, grant them first of all a deep and affectionate love for one another. Make them gentle and selfless as they care for their children, courageously guiding them through the joys and sorrows, possibilities and projects of this life. May they be strong in love for their families, always ready to forgive and begin again. Remind them, O Lord, that they can do all things through You who strengthen them. Be with them always, and bring them and their families to eternal life with You. Amen.

Consecration of Children
to Saint Joseph by Their Parents

O glorious Saint Joseph,
to you God committed the care
of His only Son
amid the many dangers of this world.
We come to you
and ask you to take under your special protection
the children God has given us.
Through Baptism they became children of God
and members of His holy Church.
We consecrate them to you today,
that through this consecration
they may become your foster children.
Guard them, guide their steps in life,
form their hearts after the hearts of Jesus and Mary.

Saint Joseph,
you felt the tribulation and worry of a parent
when the child Jesus was lost.
Protect our dear children for time and eternity.
May you be their father and counselor.
Let them, like Jesus,
grow in age as well as in wisdom and grace
before God and men.
Preserve them from the corruption of this world,
and give us the grace one day
to be united with them in heaven forever. Amen.

Litanies

Litany of the Most Holy Name of Jesus

V. Lord, have mercy. R. **Christ, have mercy.**

V. Lord, have mercy.

V. Jesus, hear us. R. **Jesus, graciously hear us.**

V. God the Father of Heaven,

R. **Have mercy on us.**

V. God the Son, Redeemer of the world,

R. **Have mercy on us.**

V. God the Holy Spirit,

R. **Have mercy on us.**

V. Holy Trinity, One God,

R. **Have mercy on us.**

R. **Have mercy on us.**

Jesus, Son of the living God,
Jesus, Splendor of the Father,
Jesus, Brightness of eternal Light,
Jesus, King of Glory,
Jesus, Sun of Justice,
Jesus, Son of the Virgin Mary,
Jesus, most amiable,
Jesus, most admirable,
Jesus, the mighty God,
Jesus, Father of the world to come,
Jesus, Angel of great counsel,
Jesus, most powerful,
Jesus, most patient,
Jesus, most obedient,
Jesus, meek and humble of heart,
Jesus, Lover of Chastity,
Jesus, our Lover,

Jesus, God of Peace,
Jesus, Author of Life,
Jesus, Model of Virtues,
Jesus, zealous for souls,
Jesus, our God,
Jesus, our Refuge,
Jesus, Father of the Poor,
Jesus, Treasure of the Faithful,
Jesus, Good Shepherd,
Jesus, true Light,
Jesus, eternal Wisdom,
Jesus, infinite Goodness,
Jesus, our Way and our Life,
Jesus, Joy of the Angels,
Jesus, King of the Patriarchs,
Jesus, Master of the Apostles,
Jesus, Teacher of the Evangelists,
Jesus, Strength of Martyrs,
Jesus, Light of Confessors,
Jesus, Purity of Virgins,
Jesus, Crown of all Saints,

V. Be merciful,   R. **Spare us, O Jesus.**
V. Be merciful,   R. **Graciously hear us, O Jesus!**

R. **Jesus, deliver us.**

From all evil,
From all sin,
From Your wrath,
From the snares of the devil,
From the spirit of fornication,
From everlasting death,
From the neglect of Your inspirations,
Through the mystery of Your Holy Incarnation,
Through Your Nativity,
Through Your Infancy,

R. Jesus, deliver us.

Through Your most divine Life,
Through Your Labors,
Through Your Agony and Passion,
Through Your Cross and dereliction,
Through Your Sufferings,
Through Your Death and Burial,
Through Your Resurrection,
Through Your Ascension,
Through Your Institution of the Most Holy Eucharist,
Through Your Joys,
Through Your Glory,

V. Lamb of God, Who takes away the sins of the world,
R. **Spare us, O Jesus!**
V. Lamb of God, Who takes away the sins of the world,
R. **Graciously hear us, O Jesus!**
V. Lamb of God, Who takes away the sins of the world,
R. **Have mercy on us, O Jesus!**
V. Jesus, hear us.
R. **Jesus, graciously hear us.**

Let us pray: Lord Jesus Christ, You have said, "Ask and you shall receive; seek and you shall find; knock and it shall be opened to you." Mercifully attend to our supplications, and grant us the grace of Your most divine love, that we may love You with all our hearts, and in all our words and actions, and never cease to praise You.

Grant us, O Lord, to have a perpetual awe and love of Your holy name, for You never fail to govern those whom You establish in Your love. We ask this of You, Who lives and reigns with Your Father and the Holy Spirit, One God, forever and ever. Amen.

Litany of the Blessed Virgin Mary

V. Lord, have mercy.   R. **Christ, have mercy.**

V. Lord, have mercy.

V. Jesus, hear us.   R. **Jesus, graciously hear us.**

V. God the Father of Heaven,

R. **Have mercy on us.**

V. God the Son, Redeemer of the world,

R. **Have mercy on us.**

V. God the Holy Spirit,

R. **Have mercy on us.**

V. Holy Trinity, One God,

R. **Have mercy on us.**

R. **Pray for us.**

Holy Mary,
Holy Mother of God,
Holy Virgin of virgins,
Mother of Christ,
Mother of divine grace,
Mother most pure,
Mother most chaste,
Mother inviolate,
Mother undefiled,
Mother most amiable,
Mother most admirable,
Mother of good counsel,
Mother of our Creator,
Mother of our Redeemer,
Mother of the Church,
Virgin most prudent,
Virgin most venerable,
Virgin most renowned,
Virgin most powerful,
Virgin most merciful,

R. **Pray for us.**

Virgin most faithful,

Mirror of justice,
Seat of wisdom,
Cause of our joy,
Spiritual vessel,
Vessel of honor,
Singular vessel of devotion,
Mystical rose,
Tower of David,
Tower of ivory,
House of gold,
Ark of the Covenant,
Gate of Heaven,
Morning star,
Health of the sick,
Refuge of sinners,
Comforter of the afflicted,
Help of Christians,
Queen of angels,
Queen of patriarchs,
Queen of prophets,
Queen of apostles,
Queen of martyrs,
Queen of confessors,
Queen of virgins,
Queen of all saints,
Queen conceived without original sin,
Queen assumed into Heaven,
Queen of the most holy Rosary,
Queen of families,
Queen of peace,

V.   Lamb of God, You take away the sins of the world,

R.   **Spare us, O Lord.**

V.   Lamb of God, You take away the sins of the world,

R.   **Graciously hear us, O Lord.**

V.   Lamb of God, You take away the sins of the world,

R.   **Have mercy on us.**

V.   Pray for us, O Holy Mother of God.

R.   **That we may be made worthy of the promises of Christ.**

Let us pray: Grant, we beseech You, O Lord God, that we Your servants may enjoy perpetual health of mind and body and by the glorious intercession of the Blessed Mary, ever Virgin, be delivered from present sorrow and enjoy eternal happiness. Through Christ, Our Lord. Amen.

Magnificat

And Mary said:

"My soul proclaims the greatness of the Lord;
   my spirit rejoices in God my savior.
For he has looked upon his handmaid's lowliness;
   behold, from now on will all ages call me blessed.
The Mighty One has done great things for me,
   and holy is his name.
His mercy is from age to age
   to those who fear him.
He has shown might with his arm,
   dispersed the arrogant of mind and heart.
He has thrown down the rulers from their thrones
   but lifted up the lowly.
The hungry he has filled with good things;
   the rich he has sent away empty.
He has helped Israel his servant,
   remembering his mercy,
according to his promise to our fathers,
   to Abraham and to his descendants forever."

–LUKE 1:45-55

Litany for the Faithful Departed

V. Lord, have mercy upon us,

R. Christ, have mercy upon us.

V. Lord, have mercy upon us,

V. God, the Father, of heaven,

R. Have mercy upon Your servants.

V. God the Son, Redeemer of the world,

R. Have mercy upon Your servants.

V. God, the Holy Spirit,

R. Have mercy upon Your servants.

V. Holy Trinity, One God.

R. Have mercy upon Your servants.

Response: **O Lord, deliver them.**

From all evil,
From Your wrath,
From the rigor of Your justice,
From eternal anguish,
By Your Incarnation,
By Your holy birth and Your sweetest Name,
By Your baptism and holy fasting,
By Your humility and obedience,
By Your poverty and meekness,
By Your love and compassion,
By Your pains and anguish,
By Your bloody sweat,
By Your scourging,
By Your crowning with thorns,
By Your cross and passion,
By Your sacred wounds,
By Your bitter death,
By Your glorious Resurrection,

By Your wonderful Ascension,
By the coming of the Holy Spirit,
In the day of judgment,

Response: **We beseech you to hear us.**

We sinners implore You to hear us.
You Who pardoned Mary Magdalene,
Who heard the prayer of the publican,
Who has the keys of death and hell,
That You would deliver the faithful departed from all the penalties of
sin,
That You would refresh and enlighten the souls of our parents,
relations, and benefactors,
That You would have mercy on the souls who are forgotten on earth,
That You would cleanse them, and be gracious to them all,
That You would fulfill their desires,
That You would bring them into the company of the Blessed,
King of tremendous majesty,

V.   Lamb of God, Who takes away the sins of the world,
R.   **Grant them rest.**
V.   Lamb of God, Who takes away the sins of the world,
R.   **Grant them eternal rest.**
V.   Lamb of God, Who takes away the sins of the world,
R.   **Have mercy upon them.**

Let us pray: We beseech You, O Lord, to grant perpetual light to the
souls of Your servants; that their faith and hope in You may avail to
their eternal salvation. Through Christ our Lord. Amen.

Litany of Saint Joseph

V. Lord, have mercy on us.
R. **Christ, have mercy on us.**
V. Lord, have mercy on us.
V. Christ, hear us.
R. **Christ, graciously hear us.**

God the Father of Heaven,
R. **Have mercy on us.**
God the Son, Redeemer of the world,
R. **Have mercy on us.**
God the Holy Spirit,
R. **Have mercy on us.**
Holy Trinity, one God,
R. **Have mercy on us.**

Response: **Pray for us.**

Holy Mary,
Saint Joseph,
Renowned offspring of David,
Light of Patriarchs,
Spouse of the Mother of God,
Chaste guardian of the Virgin,
Foster father of the Son of God,
Diligent protector of Christ,
Head of the Holy Family,
Joseph most just,
Joseph most chaste,
Joseph most prudent,
Joseph most strong,
Joseph most obedient,
Joseph most faithful,

Mirror of patience,
Lover of poverty,
Model of artisans,
Glory of home life,
Guardian of virgins,
Pillar of families,
Solace of the wretched,
Hope of the sick,
Patron of the dying,
Terror of demons,
Protector of Holy Church,

V.   Lamb of God, Who takes away the sins of the world,
R.   **Spare us, O Lord.**
V.   Lamb of God, Who takes away the sins of the world,
R.   **Graciously hear us, O Lord.**
V.   Lamb of God, Who takes away the sins of the world,
R.   **Have mercy on us.**

V.   He made him the lord of his household.
R.   **And prince over all his possessions.**

Let us pray: O God, in Your ineffable providence You were pleased to choose Blessed Joseph to be the spouse of Your most holy Mother; grant, we beg You, that we may be worthy to have him for our intercessor in heaven whom on earth we venerate as our Protector: You who live and reign forever and ever. Amen.

OUR LADY
OF THE ROSARY

MARY,
QUEEN OF THE MOST HOLY ROSARY,
PRAY FOR US.